WHAT IS ISLAM?

by Nahida Esmail

© Nahida Esmail

Written by Nahida Esmail

Layout and illustrations by Rey Of Light Design

Edited by Khadijah Stott-Andrew

Contents

3 Who are you?
4 What is Islam?
6 What do Muslims believe?
8 Why did God Create Mankind?
10 Who is Allah?
12 What is the Qur'an?
14 What are the five pillars?
16 First Pillar - Testimony of Faith
18 Second Pillar - Prayer
20 How Do Muslims Pray?
22 What is a Masjid?
24 Third Pillar - Charity
26 Fourth Pillar - Fasting
28 What is Eid-ul-Fitr?
30 Fifth Pillar - Pilgrimage
32 What is Eid-ul-Adha?
33 Abraham's Sacrifice
34 Who were the Prophets?
36 Do Muslims Believe in Jesus?
38 Who was Muhammad (peace be upon him)?
40 What did Muhammad (peace be upon him) say?
42 What do Christianity and Islam Have in Common?
44 Common Arabic Phrases
46 Top Facts
47 Famous Muslims
48 Activities
52 Quiz
54 Answers

Who Are You?

This book belongs to:

Name: ....

Age: ....

My religion is: ....

My school is called: ....
....

Did You Know?
Both Christianity and Islam started in the Middle East.

What is Islam?

Islam is to peacefully submit to the will and guidance of God.

"The true religion in the sight of Allah is Islam" *(The Qur'an - 3:19)*

Islam's holy book is called The Qur'an.

Muhammad (peace be upon him) was Islam's last and final prophet.

Who is Islam for?
Islam is a religion for all of mankind. People of all races, nations and colours are Muslim.

Who are Muslims?
A Muslim is a follower of Islam and submits to God's commands.

How should Muslims behave?
- Live healthily
- Respect your parents
- Treat your neighbors well
- Talk politely
- Be clean
- Help others
- Be kind

Islam is an Arabic word which means "peace" and "submission to God"

Did You Know?

Islam is not a new religion. It was the religion of all the Prophets before Muhammad (peace be upon him), including Adam, Abraham, Noah, Moses and Jesus (peace be upon them all).

All of them brought the same message from God.

How do you become a Muslim?

If someone wants to become a Muslim, they must believe and say:

"There is no god worthy of worship but Allah and Muhammad is the Messenger of Allah".

This is known as the *shahadah*, the first pillar of Islam.

What do Muslims believe?

Islam teaches Muslims to believe in six pillars of faith:
1. Allah (God)
2. Angels
3. Messengers
4. Holy books
5. The Day of Judgment
6. God's Will.

Who is Allah?

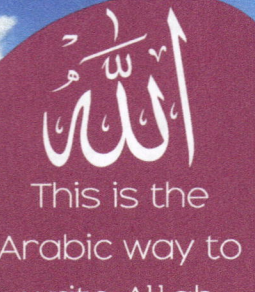

This is the Arabic way to write Allah

"Allah is the Creator of all things."
(The Qur'an - 39:62)

Allah is the one true God.

Only Allah has the power to create and He is the Creator of all things.

Bible or Qur'an?

Can you match the verse to the correct holy book?

"Say, 'He is God the One. God the eternal. He does not reproduce, nor was He born. No one is comparable to Him.'"

"And Jesus answered him, the first of all the commandments is, Hear O Israel; The Lord our God is one Lord"

The Qur'an - chapter 112

Mark 12:29

Isaiah 44:6

Why Did God Create Mankind?

God says in the Qur'an:

"I created jinn and mankind only to worship Me"
(The Qur'an - 51:56)

Muslims believe that the purpose of life is to worship God, the Creator of all things.

What is worship in Islam?

Many actions can be classed as worship:
- Being aware of God and obeying His commands.
- Being kind to animals.
- Helping your mother
- Speaking nicely about people
- Fasting
- Praying

Circle the acts of worship

Praying
Reading Qur'an
Being clean
Fasting
Helping your mother

What is the Qur'an?

Muslims believe the Qur'an is the last book sent down by Allah in His own words.

It was revealed in Arabic to the Prophet Muhammed (peace be upon him) through the Archangel Gabriel.

The Qur'an was sent down to guide all of mankind to the truth. Not a single word has been added to the Qur'an, nor has any word or verse been removed from it.

Which holy book did each prophet receive?

The Torah   The Psalms   The Gospel   The Qur'an

   Muhammad   David   Moses   Jesus
(peace be upon them all)

Did You Know?

Four holy books were sent to mankind and they all had the same message. Over time, these messages were distorted, so Allah promised to protect the final message - The Qur'an.

"It was in the month of Ramadan that the Qur'an was revealed as guidance for mankind, clear messages giving guidance and distinguishing between right and wrong. So any one of you who sees in that month should fast, and anyone who is ill or on a journey should make up for the lost days by fasting on other days later." (The Qur'an 2:185)

What are the Five Pillars?

Islam is built on five pillars. This means Muslims must believe in and practice 5 things:

1. Believe in one God and believe Muhammad (peace be upon him) is His messenger. This is called *Shahadah*.
2. Pray to God five times a day. This is called *Salah*.
3. Fast during the month of Ramadan. This is called *Sawm*.
4. Give to charity. This is called *Zakah*.
5. Go on a pilgrimage to Makkah once in their lifetime. This is called *Hajj*.

"Islam is to bear witness that there is none worthy of worship except Allah and that Muhammad is the Messenger of Allah; to establish the Prayer; to pay the Zakah (charity); to fast in the month of Ramadan; and to perform the pilgrimage to The House if he is capable of travel." *(Muslim)*

The 1st Pillar: Testimony of Faith

The most important pillar of Islam is the testimony of faith. This means a Muslim must believe firmly and say the following:

La ilaha illAllah wa-Muhammadan rasulAllah.

There is no god but Allah and Muhammad is the Messenger of Allah.

The Shahaadah has two parts:
   There is none worthy of worship except Allah.
This means that Muslims must only worship Allah.

2. *Muhammad is the Messenger of Allah.*
This means that Muslims must believe that Allah sent Muhammad as the final Messenger.

Did You Know?

This was the same message given by Jesus (peace be upon him). A Jew came to him and asked, "what is the first commandment?" Jesus replied, "Hear, oh Isra'il, the Lord our God is one God (He has no partner)."

(Mark 12:29)

Shahadah is the Arabic word for the testimony of faith. Every Muslim must believe and say the shahadah.

The 2nd Pillar: Prayer

Muslims have been commanded to pray five times a day and each prayer has a special name.

Fajr: This is the dawn prayer, performed before sunrise.

Dhuhr: This is the midday prayer.

'Asr: This is the afternoon prayer.

Maghrib: This is the sunset prayer.

'Isha: This is the evening prayer.

Did You Know?

Muslims used to face Jerusalem for their prayers, but Allah told Prophet Muhammad (peace be upon him) to tell the Muslims to face Makkah instead.

The Ka'bah is the first House of God built by Abraham and his son Ismail (peace be upon them).

> The prayer helps Muslims to remember Allah and feel closer to Him. When they pray, Muslims face the direction of the Ka'bah in Makkah.

Bible or Qur'an?
Can you guess where this verse is from?

"Going a little farther, he (Jesus peace be upon him) fell with his face to the ground and prayed, "My Father, if it is possible, may this cup be taken from me. Yet not as I will, but as you will."

How Do Muslims Pray?

Muslims must be in a clean state when they pray, so they perform 'ablution' and wash themselves.

Ablution is also mentioned in the New and Old Testament:
"Then David got up from the ground. After he had washed, put on lotions and changed his clothes, he went into the house of the Lord and worshiped …" *(Samuel 12:20 - New International Version (NIV))*

Ablution in the Qur'an:
"You who believe, when you are about to pray, wash your faces and your hands and arms up to the elbows, wipe your heads, wash your feet up to your ankles," *(The Qur'an - 5:6)*

Did You Know?

The true position of prayer for the Christians is the same as the Muslims - to prostrate during prayer by resting their faces on the ground. The Christian Scripture describes Jesus (peace be upon him) as praying with his head bowed to the ground, just like Muslims.

Prostrating during prayer was also practiced by Moses, Abraham, David and others.

The positions of Prayer

1. Face the direction of the Ka'bah. The Prophet Muhammad (peace be upon him) said: "The Prophet said, "When you get up for the prayer, perform the ablution properly and then face the Qiblah and say Takbir (Allahu Akbar)" *(Bukhari)*

2. Recite verses from the Qur'an whilst standing.

3. Put your hands on your knees and bow. This is known as *Rukoo*. The Prophet Muhammad said, "Bow, place the palms on the knees; spread the fingers and remain still until every limb rests into its position." *(Ibn Hib-ban)*

4. Lower your forehead to the ground in prostration. This is known as *sujood*. The Prophet Muhammad (peace be upon him) used to keep his arms away from his body while performing sujood." *(Agreed upon)*

5. Lift your forehead and remain knelt on the ground. This is known as *Tashahud*.

6. Turn your face to the right and then the left and say both times, "Asalamuaikum wa rahmatu Allah" (Peace be with you by the Mercy of Allah). This is known as 'making Tasliem.'

Wudhu
eans 'ablution'.
t is the special
y Muslims wash
emselves before
they pray.

What is a Masjid?

A mosque is a place of worship, like a church.

However, Muslims can pray almost anywhere, such as on the beach, fields, parking lots, offices, etc.

The masjid is always kept very clean for people to pray in. There are usually separate sections for men and women. When people go into the masjid, they take off their shoes to keep the ground clean to pray on.

"When he came to the Fire, he was called: 'Moses! I am your Lord. Take off your shoes: you are in the sacred valley of Tuwa." *(The Qur'an - 20: 11-12)*

(And God said to Moses) "Draw not nigh hither: put off thy shoes from thy feet, for the place whereon thou standest is holy ground." *(Exodus 3:5, also ACTS 7:33)*

What do you think Muslims should do when they go to the masjid? Tick your answers.

- ☐ High five people
- ☐ Make wudhu
- ☐ Remove their shoes
- ☐ Keep the masjid clean
- ☐ Whistle
- ☐ Play games
- ☐ Greet everyone nicely
- ☐ Wear clean clothes

Masjid is the Arabic word for 'mosque', a place of worship.

Did You Know?
The three most important masjids are:
1. The mosque where the Ka'bah is in Makkah, Saudi Arabia.
2. The Prophet's mosque in Madinah, Saudi Arabia
3. The Al-Aqsa mosque in Jerusalem, Palestine.

The 3rd Pillar: Charity

Each year, Muslims should give a small amount* of their wealth to the poor.

Giving to charity shows that Muslims care for one another and help those in need.

Bible or Qur'an?

Can you match the verse to the correct holy book?

"[People], keep up the prayer, pay the prescribed alms (charity)."

"But when you give to the needy, do not let your left hand know what your right hand is doing, so that your giving may be in secret..".

"Give generously to them and do so without a grudging heart; then because of this the Lord your God will bless you in all your work and in everything you put your hand to. There will always be poor people in the land. Therefore, I command you to be openhanded toward your fellow Israelites who are poor and needy in your land."

The Qur'an - 24:56
Deuteronomy 15:10-11
Matthew 6:3-4

*2.5%

The 4th Pillar:
Fasting

Ramadan is the 9th month of the Islamic calendar.

Muslims must fast every day for the entire month of Ramadan. They do not eat or drink from dawn until sunset.

Fasting helps a Muslim to be thankful for what he has and Allah forgives the sins of those who fast.

Did Allah's messengers fast?

Moses fasted for forty days in preparation for receiving the Ten Commandments *(Exodus - 34:28)*.
Daniel fasted for three weeks before receiving his vision *(Daniel - 10:2-6)*.
Elijah fasted forty days before speaking with God *(1 Kings - 19:8)*.

What are the benefits of fasting?

Lots of scientific research has found that fasting:
- Improves your resistance to disease
- Helps you sleep better
- Helps you to develop good habits
- Clears your skin
- Helps with allergies
- Gives you energy
- Provides rest for your digestive organs
- Helps you to lose weight
- Helps your body get rid of toxins
- May reduce the risk of heart disease and diabetes.

Sahoor is the meal Muslims eat early in the morning before fasting.

Iftaar is the meal Muslims eat after sunset when they break their fast.

Did You Know?
The Christian Scripture shows that fasting increases one's faith. If you do not pray and fast then you will not have faith, and if you don't have faith then you will not enter paradise.

Sawm is the Arabic word for 'fasting'.

Bible or Qur'an?
Can you match the verse to the correct holy book?

"You will not have faith except by prayer and fasting."

"O you who believe, fasting is prescribed for you, as it was prescribed for those before you, so that you may become pious."

The Qur'an - 2:183

Matthew 17: 18-20

Eid-ul-Fitr

The day after the month of Ramadan, Muslims celebrate Eid-ul-Fitr.

Muslims celebrate with a special prayer in the morning at the mosque whilst wearing their best clothes.

They rejoice for the rest of the day with friends and relatives by sharing good food, giving presents and giving to charity.

Draw a picture of what you would like to receive as a present, inside the gift box.

The 5th Pillar:
Pilgrimage

When Muslims perform Hajj, they go to Makkah in Saudi Arabia during the Islamic month of Dhul-Hijjah and perform certain rituals.

If Hajj is performed correctly, it will wipe away all of your past sins.

Muslims learn true unity from Hajj because everyone is dressed the same and worshipping Allah together.

"Pilgrimage to the House is a duty owed to God by people who are able to undertake it. Those who reject this [should know that] God has no need of anyone."
-The Qur'an 3:97

"Blessed are those who dwell in your house; they are ever praising you."
- Psalms/84:4 (New International version)

When Muslims visit the Ka'bah, they circle it seven times, whilst reciting prayers to Allah.

Hajj is the Arabic word Muslims use to mean the pilgrimage to Makkah.

Eid-ul-Adha

Eid-ul-Adha is also known as the 'Greater Eid' or 'Festival of Sacrifice' and is celebrated at the end of the Hajj pilgrimage.

A special prayer is read in the morning at mosques around the world. Goats, sheep, cows and/or camels are sacrificed to remember the time when Abraham was going to sacrifice his own son Ishmael to prove obedience to Allah. The meat from the sacrifices is shared amongst family, friends and the poor.

Bible or Qur'an?
Can you match the verse to the correct holy book?

Then God said, "Take your son, your only son, whom you love, Isaac, and go to the region of Moriah. Sacrifice him there as a burnt offering on a mountain I will show you."

"When the boy was old enough to work with his father, Abraham said, 'My son, I have seen myself sacrificing you in a dream. What do you think?' He said, 'Father, do as you are commanded and, God willing, you will find me steadfast.'"

The Qur'an - 37:102

Genesis - 22:2 New International Version

Abraham's Sacrifice

During Eid-ul-Adha, Muslims offer a special sacrifice of an animal.

They do this to remember the command given to Prophet Abraham.

This is Allah's way of teaching Muslims to follow the path of Abraham who was keen to sacrifice what was dearest to him for Allah (i.e. his son). We should learn from this and always be willing to give what is beloved to us for the sake of Allah.

Qurbani is the Arabic word for 'sacrifice'.

Did You Know?
The story of Abraham is also found in the Christian Old Testament (Genesis 22). However, in the Old Testament, God asked Abraham to sacrifice his other son, Isaac.

Who Were the Prophets?

Muslims believe that approximately 124,000 prophets were sent by Allah to guide mankind, but only 25 are mentioned in the Qur'an. Prophet Muhammad (peace be upon him) was the final and greatest of them. All prophets brought the same message from God to humankind: *believe in the one true God, Allah.*

Can you match up the biblical names with the correct Arabic names?

Arabic Name	Biblical Name
Adam	Abraham
Ayub	Ishmael
Dawood	Enoch
Harun	Jesus
Hud	David
Ibrahim	Zachariah
Idris	Isaac
Ilyas	Aaron
Isa	Lot
Ishaq	Jacob
Isma'il	Adam
Lut	John
Musa	Noah
Nuh	Joseph
Sulaiman	Job
Ya'qub	Hud
Yahya	Jonah
Yunus	Elijah
Yusuf	Moses
Zakariyah	Solomon

"So [you believers], say, 'We believe in God and in what was sent down to us and what was sent down to Abraham. Ishmael, Isaac, Jacob, and the Tribes, and what was given to Moses, Jesus, and all the prophets by their Lord. We make no distinction between any of them, and we devote ourselves to Him.'

-The Qur'an - 2:136

Did You Know?

Muslims believe in a lot of the same prophets as Christians. In the Qur'an, the prophets' names are in Arabic.

Do Muslims Believe in Jesus?

Muslims believe Jesus was a prophet and messenger of Allah, not the son of God or God Himself. Allah sent Jesus with a holy book called the Gospel (or *Injeel* in Arabic). Jesus was sent to confirm the messages of all the prophets before him.

Muslims love Jesus respect him as a great prophet of God. Jesus' mother was called Mary and she was a pure and pious believer in Allah. Muslims believe Jesus was born miraculously without a father.

Bible or Qur'an?
Can you match the verse to the correct holy book?

"In God's eyes, Jesus is just like Adam: He created him from dust, said to him, 'Be', and he was."

"Do not think that I have come to abolish the Law or the Prophets; I have not come to abolish them but to fulfill them."

The Qur'an - 3:59

Matthew - 5:17 New International Version

Did Jesus Perform Miracles?

Allah gave Jesus many miracles. The Qur'an tells us Jesus (peace be upon him) was able to speak when he was a baby in his cradle. Jesus would defend his mother, Mary, when the people asked her where the baby came from. *"...Peace was on me the day I was born, and will be on me the day I die and the day I am raised to life again.' Such was Jesus, son of Mary."* -The Qur'an - 19:30-34

Jesus also prayed to Allah to send down a table spread with food when his disciples asked him to. With Allah's help and permission, Jesus also healed the blind and lepers and even brought the dead back to life. The Qur'an also tells us that Jesus (peace be upon him) said, "I have come to you with a sign from your Lord: I make the shape of a bird for you out of clay, then breathe into it and, with God's permission; it will become a real bird; I will heal the blind and the leper, and bring the dead back to life with God's permission." -The Qur'an 3:49

Jesus will return

Muslims believe that Jesus was not crucified or resurrected. They believe Jesus was raised up to the heavens whilst he was still alive and one day he will return towards the end of time.
-The Qur'an - 4: 157-158

Who Was Muhammad (peace be upon him)?

In 610 C.E, Allah sent Angel Gabriel to Muhammad (peace be upon him) with the first divine message of the Qur'an. For the next 23 years, Muhammad continued to receive revelations until the Qur'an was complete. Muhammad (peace be upon him) asked people to believe in one God and be kind and merciful to one another. He was a living example of God's guidance for all of mankind to follow.

Are these facts about Muhammad (peace be upon him) true or false?

1. Muhammad was the last and final prophet.
2. Muhammad lived in Egypt.
3. He was an orphan.
4. He was known as 'Al-Amin' meaning 'The Truthful', because he never told a lie.
5. His father was also a prophet.

At the mention of the Prophet's name

When Muslims hear the Prophets name they should say, "May the peace and blessings of Allah be upon him". They say this out of respect for him.

Did You Know?

Muhammed is mentioned by name in songs of Solomon (5:16). The Hebrew word used is "Mahummudim".

Bible or Qur'an?

Can you match the verse to the correct holy book?

"Then We revealed to you [Muhammad], 'Follow the creed of Abraham, a man of pure faith who was not an idolater.'"

"I have much more to say to you, more than you can now bear. But when he, the Spirit of truth, comes, he will guide you into all the truth. He will not speak on his own; he will speak only what he hears, and he will tell you what is yet to come. He will glorify me because it is from me that he will receive what he will make known to you."

The Qur'an - 16:123

John/16:12-14

What did Prophet Muhammad (peace be upon him) teach?

The *hadith* include:
1. Things Muhammad (peace be upon him) said.
2. His actions.
3. Examples of things that happened around him and his response.

The Prophet Muhammad (peace be upon him) would also explain to his companions what the verses of the Qur'an meant, giving them a detailed explanation of Allah's word.

In the Qur'an, Allah commands us to follow Muhammad's prophetic message:

"...so accept whatever the Messenger gives you, and abstain from whatever he forbids you."
- The Qur'an - 59:7

Hadith is the Arabic word for the teachings of Muhammad (peace be upon him). Hadith are the second source of Islamic law, after the Qur'an.

How do we know what the hadith are?

The companions of Prophet Muhammad (peace be upon him) used to memorize things he said and did, and they would write them down. These writings have been passed down over the years and have been carefully checked by scholars. Now we have collections of books with all the correct hadith for us to read.

Qur'an and Hadith - What's the difference?

Qur'an
- The speech of Allah.
- Given to Muhammad (peace be upon him) by Angel Gabriel.
- Muhammad (peace be upon him) then passed this on to his companions and followers.

Hadith
- The speech and actions of Muhammad (peace be upon him).
- Some explanations of the Qur'an.

What do Christianity and Islam have in common?

Islam and Christianity are very similar, because both their messengers were sent by the one God, Allah.

ISLAM

- Muslims believe in one God.
- Muslims perform ablution before prayers.
- Muslims remove their shoes when they enter a place of worship.
- A Muslim woman covers her head.
- Muslims call God by His Arabic name, Allah.

CHRISTIANITY

- Christians believe in one God.
- In the Bible, abulution before prayers is encouraged.
- Moses was told to remove his shoes when he was standing on holy ground.
- In the Bible, women are told to cover their heads.
- In the Arabic text of the Bible, *Allah* is used to refer to God.

Common Arabic phrases

Assalaamu Alaikum - *May peace be upon you.*
Muslims say this when they greet each other.

MashaAllah (Ma – Sha – Al- Lahh) - *It is as Allah wills.*
Muslims say this when they see something beautiful or hear some good news.

InshaAllah - *If Allah wills.*
Muslims say this if they want to do something in the future. This reminds them that Allah is in control of everything.

Alhamdulilah - *Praise be to Allah.*
Muslims say this when they are thankful for something.

Bismillah - *In the name of Allah.*
Muslims say this when they start a task, such as eating. *Bismillah* is also the beginning of most of the chapters in the Qur'an.

Allahu Akbar - *God is the Greatest.*
Muslims can say this at any time. It is often used in celebration or after a great achievement.

SubhanAllah - *Glory be to Allah.*
Muslims say this when they are amazed at something. Saying this praises God and all His attributes.

Top facts

- Muslims love Jesus (peace be upon him) and all the other prophets sent by God.

- Mary, the mother of Jesus (peace be upon him) and other women around him wore a scarf, just like Muslim women do.

"Rebekah also looked up and saw Isaac. She got down from her camel and asked the servant, 'Who is that man in the field coming to meet us?' "He is my master," the servant answered. So she took her veil and covered herself. [Genesis 24: 64-65 - New International Version (NIV)]

"But every woman who prays or prophesies with her head uncovered dishonors her head - it is the same as having her head shaved." [Corinthians 11:5 - New International Version (NIV)]

- Jesus (peace be upon him) placed his face on the ground in prostration to God, just like Muslims do.

- Being Muslim means you submit yourself to God.

- Jesus (peace be upon him) spoke Aramic, which is close to Arabic.

- There is a chapter in the Qur'an called 'Maryam' or 'Mary'. This chapter tells us about Jesus (peace be upon him) and his mother.

- Muslims don't eat pork. The Bible also prohibits pork.
"And the pig, though it has a divided hoof, does not chew the cud; it is unclean for you. You must not eat their meat or touch their carcasses; they are unclean for you." [Leviticus 11:7-8 - New International Version (NIV)]

Famous Muslims

Did you know these famous people are Muslim?
Mohammed Ali
Mike Tyson
Amir Khan (boxer)
Cat Stevens (now known as Yusuf Islam)
Yusuf Chambers
Jermaine Jackson
Shaquille O'Neal
Professor Salim S. AbdoolKarim
Yvonne Ridley
Sayeeda Warsi
Malala Yousafzai
Hakeem Olajuwon
Khaled Hosseini

Wordsearch

```
A O P B C E M U H A M M A D O P
G N I T S A F F E Q R A S Y O T
S T L M A C D A Q U X L S R U S
W M G D E N O W R V H K M J E Z
H Q R B C H P G N E E O E I I N
A U I E I A L L A H P S J W D D
D R M P F J B F O Q U E R M X S A
A S A C I J D N O S V F T C Z X
H T G C R B J M L R M U O H P Q
A L E D C I A K A M Q L N A Y O
H E H I A L J L P R A Y E R N R
S F B F S X G W J N Y K F I Y P
A G P I E I Y C V O D U T T S X
L S H Q B H B I N G I E Z Y L M
B U J G D L S T Z O N A R U Q W
K M R T C G E A H K U X O V O V
```

ALLAH
MUHAMMAD
JESUS
SHAHADAH

MASJID
ISLAM
PRAYER
CHARITY

MARY
HAJJ
FASTING
BIBLE

QURAN
EID
SACRIFICE
PILGRIMAGE

Spot the similarities
Can you circle the similarities between this nun and Muslim woman?

Quiz

List 3 things you know about Islam and Muslims:

Who was Muhammad? List 3 things you know about him:

The Qur'an is the word of

_____

How do Muslims fast during Ramadan?

What do Muslims believe about Jesus?

Where do Muslims face when they pray?

Muslims believe they are created to:

_____

How many times a day do Muslims pray?

Answers

Page 8: Who is Allah?
Bible or Qur'an?
"And Jesus answered him, the first of all the commandments is, Hear O Israel; The Lord our God is one Lord" - **Mark 12:29**

"I am the first and I am the last; besides Me there is no god." - **Isaiah 44:6**

"Say, 'He is God the One. God the eternal. He does not reproduce, nor was He born. No one is comparable to Him. - **The Qur'an - chapter 112**

Circle things created by Allah.
Allah created everything!

Page 10: Why did God create mankind?
Circle the acts of worship.
- Reading the Qur'an
- Helping your mother
- Being clean
- Praying
- Fasting
- Feeding animals

Page 12: What is the Qur'an?
Which holy book did each prophet receive?
The Torah - Prophet Moses
The Psalms - Prophet David
The Gospel - Prophet Jesus
The Qur'an - Prophet Muhammad
(Peace be upon them all)

Page 18: 2nd Pillar - Prayer
Bible or Qur'an?
"Going a little farther, he (Jesus peace be upon him) fell with his face to the ground and prayed, "My Father, if it is possible, may this cup be taken from me. Yet not as I will, but as you will." - **Matthew/26:39 - New International Version**

Page 22: What is a Masjid?
What do you think Muslims should do when they go to the masjid?
- Make wudhu
- Remove their shoes
- Keep the masjid clean
- Greet everyone nicely
- Wear clean clothes

Page 24: 3rd Pillar - Charity
Bible or Qur'an?
"[People], keep up the prayer, pay the prescribed alms (charity)." - **The Qur'an - 24:56**

"Give generously to them and do so without a grudging heart; then because of this the Lord your God will bless you in all your work and in everything you put your hand to. There will always be poor people in the land. Therefore, I command you to be openhanded toward your fellow Israelites who are poor and needy in your land" - **Deuteronomy 15:10-11 - New International Version (NIV)**

"But when you give to the needy, do not let your left hand know what your right hand is doing, so that your giving may be in secret." - **Matthew 6:3-4 - New International Version (NIV)**

Page 26: 4th Pillar - Fasting
Bible or Qur'an?
"O you who believe, fasting is prescribed for you, as it was prescribed for those before you, so that you may become pious." - **The Qur'an - 2:183**
"You will not have faith except by prayer and fasting" - **Mathew 17: 18-20**

Page 32: Eid ul-Adha
Bible or Qur'an
"When the boy was old enough to work with his father, Abraham said, 'My son, I have seen myself sacrificing you in a dream. What do you think?' He said, 'Father, do as you are commanded, and, God willing, you will find me steadfast.'" - **The Qur'an - 37:102**

"Then God said, 'Take your son, your only son, whom you love, Isaac, and go to the region of Moriah. Sacrifice him there as a burnt offering on a mountain I will show you.'" - **Genesis 22:2 - New International Version (NIV)**

Page 34: Who were the Prophets?

Can you write the correct biblical name next to the Arabic name?

Adam - Adam
Ayub - Job
Dawood - David
Harun - Aaron
Hud - Hud
Ibrahim - Abraham
Idris - Enoch
Ilyas - Elijah
Isa - Jesus
Ishaq - Issac
Isma'il - Ishmael
Lut - Lot
Musa - Moses
Nuh - Noah
Sulaiman - Solomon
Ya'qub - Jacob
Yahya - John
Yunus - Jonah
Yusuf - Joseph
Zakariyah - Zachariah

*Peace and blessings upon all the prophets.

Page 36: Do Muslims believe in Jesus?

Bible or Qur'an?

"In God's eyes, Jesus is just like Adam: He created him from dust, said to him, 'Be', and he was." - **The Qur'an 3:59**

"Do not think that I have come to abolish the Law or the Prophets; I have not come to abolish them but to fulfill them." - **Matthew 5:17 (New International Version (NIV)**

Page 38: Who was Muhammad (peace be upon him)?

Are these facts about Muhammad (peace be upon him) true or false?
1. Muhammad was the last and final prophet. TRUE.
2. Muhammad lived in Egypt. FALSE.
3. He was an orphan. TRUE.

4. He was known as 'Al-Amin' meaning 'The Truthful', because he never told a lie. TRUE.
5. His father was also a prophet. FALSE.

Bible or Qur'an?
"I have much more to say to you, more than you can now bear. 13 But when he, the Spirit of truth, comes, he will guide you into all the truth. He will not speak on his own; he will speak only what he hears, and he will tell you what is yet to come. 14 He will glorify me because it is from me that he will receive what he will make known to you." - **John/16:12-14 - New International Version (NIV)**

"Then We revealed to you [Muhammad], 'Follow the creed of Abraham, a man of pure faith who was not an idolater.'" - **The Qur'an - 16:123**

Page 48: Spot the difference

Page 50: Word search

Page 51: Spot the similarities

1. Head covering
2. Holy book
3. Prayer beads
4. Place of worship

Both Muslims and Christians follow their holy book for guidance. Some Muslims use a 'tasbeeh' which are just like rosary beads to help them keep count of their prayers. When a Christian woman submits herself to God and becomes a nun, she often wears a head covering, just like the hijab a Muslim woman wears. Although you can't see it, both Muslims and Christians have a love for God in their hearts.

Page 52: Quiz

List 3 things you know about Islam and Muslims.
(i) 'Islam' is an Arabic word which means 'peace' and 'Submission to God'.
(ii) Muslims believe that the Qur'an is the last book sent down by Allah.
(iii) Muslims don't eat pork.
OR anything else from the text.

Who was Muhammad? List 3 things you know about him.
(i) Muhammed is the last messenger sent by Allah to mankind.
(ii) He received revelation from Allah.
(iii) He was known as 'the truthful'.
OR anything else from the text.

What do Muslims believe about Jesus?
Muslims believe Jesus was one of the Prophets sent by Allah.

The Qur'an is the word of _____
The Qur'an is the word of Allah.

How do Muslims fast during Ramadan?
Muslims fast during Ramadan by not eating or drinking from dawn until sunset.

Where do Muslims face when they pray?
Muslims face towards the Ka'bah in Makkah when they pray.

How many times a day do Muslims pray?
Muslims pray 5 times a day.

Muslims believe they are created to_____
Muslims believe they are created to worship God.

www.ingramcontent.com/pod-product-compliance
Lightning Source LLC
Chambersburg PA
CBHW052131010526
44113CB00034B/1868